Forex Trading For Beginners

Forex Trading For Beginners

A Basic Guide to Mastery in Forex Trading

ELLEN LEVESQUE

Copyright © 2019 by Ellen Levesque. All rights reserved.

No piece of this distribution might be replicated, transmitted in any platform or using any means, photocopying, recording, filtering, electronic, or something else, without authorization recorded as a hard copy from the distributor.

Consenting to see this material or to utilize the substance inside this book you concur this is a general training material and you won't consider anyone answerable for misfortune or harms coming about because of the substance given here including the distributor.

Don't COPY!!!!

THE TREND IS YOUR FRIEND UNTIL THE END

Contents

ACKNOWLEDGMENT 13
DEDICATION 15
INTRODUCTION 17
PART 1 19
FOREX 19
BASICS 19
CHAPTER 1   HISTORY OF FOREX 21
CHAPTER 2 27
MAJOR MARKET PARTICIPANTS 27
CHAPTER 3 33
WHAT IS FOREX 33
CHAPTER 4 37
WHAT IS TRADED IN 37
THE FOREX MARKET 37
CHAPTER 5 47
WHEN TO TRADE FOREX 47
CHAPTER 6 59
BUYING VS SELLING 59
PART 2 63
TRADING TERMS 63
CHAPTER 7 65
WHAT ARE PIPS AND HOW THEY ARE CALCULATED 65

CHAPTER 8 77
WHAT ARE LEVERAGE AND LOTS..........77
CHAPTER 9 81
YOUR TRADING WINDOW..........................81
CHAPTER 10 85
TYPES OF ORDERS 85
PART 3 91
ANALYZING THE FOREX MARKET 91
CHAPTER 11 93
THREE TYPES OF ANALYSIS.....................93
CHAPTER 12 97
WHAT IS A TREND..97
CHAPTER 13 107
WHAT IS PRICE ACTION...........................107
CHAPTER 14 111
SUPPORT,..111
RESISTANCE AND TRENDLINES 111
CHAPTER 15 115
WHAT IS A PULLBACK 115
CHAPTER 16 119
CONFIRMATION CHECKLIST 119
PART 4 125
RISK AND MONEY MANAGEMENT 125

CHAPTER 17 127
TRADING PLAN 127
CHAPTER 18 135
RISK MANAGEMENT PART 1 135
CHAPTER 19 139
RISK MANAGEMENT PART 2 139
CONCLUSION 143

ACKNOWLEDGMENT

Many people who deserve acknowledgment for this book, most especially my sister for always being there for me. I also acknowledge all those traders and friends who have provided help, criticism, and ideas over the past years.

I hope this book will start a new wave of fruitful discussion that will benefit all traders out there.

DEDICATION

It is with the sincerest honor that I dedicate this book to all the traders out there especially the beginners. I believe you would be successful if you take the time to read this book.

INTRODUCTION

Forex, which is the short form for foreign exchange has to do with the exchange of currencies around the world, which involves the banks, private and public investors, retail traders, and the Government.
This market functions differently from the stock market; the stock market has a fixed daily schedule for opening and closing, whereas forex is open 24hrs a day, five days a week nonstop.

The main market involves in the forex are Newyork, London, Sydney, Tokyo, Frankfurt. The forex market is the largest market in the world where $3.2 trillion is transacted every day. When you are transacting in the forex market you are simultaneously buying one currency and selling another. Currencies are always traded in pairs, for example, USDCAD, GBPUSD, XAUUSD, Currency trading used to be exclusively for the central banks, government, rich investors and the hedgers. But all thanks to the internet, retail traders can trade the forex market.

PART 1
FOREX BASICS

CHAPTER 1
HISTORY OF FOREX

OVERVIEW
- What is a bartering system?
- Why was the bartering system so flawed?
- What was the commodity system?
- Why was the conversion of a coin so significant?
- How did paper money come about?
- What was the gold standard?
- What is the floating exchange rate system?

BARTERING SYSTEM

The immediate trade of one commodity or service for another without the utilization of cash is named "Barter System". In this framework, cash doesn't exist.
- ➢ This involves the exchange of goods for services. Example: Livestock, Skills, Talents, People, and Salt.
- ➢ They traded things they didn't need for things they needed.

Fig 1.1

DISADVANTAGES OF THE BARTERING SYSTEM
1. Having something that no one wanted
2. Limited shelf life
3. Transportation and storage
4. Fair exchange(They will have to agree before an exchange can be done)
5. Hard to repay debt.

Due to the disadvantage, it was abandoned for a more intermediate commodity system.

COMMODITY SYSTEM

- Ancient China, Africa, and India used cowry shells.
- In Japan, it was based on koku(a unit of rice)
- The shekel was a specific weight of barley.

Fig 1.2

COINAGE

These coins were made from electrum (a mixture of silver and gold that occurs naturally).This was used as a means of exchange.

Fig 1.3

ADVANTAGES
1. People could naturally trade what they wanted for what they needed.
2. Coins were easier to transport.

DISADVANTAGES
1. Coins' weight could change over time (due to wear and tear).
2. Coins could be counterfeited.
3. Coins were very heavy to carry.

PAPER MONEY

Paper money is a medium of exchange for goods and services within an economy. It is printed in paper. This is the most generally accepted form of exchange.

Fig 1.4

- The Chinese invented paper money in the form of notes in 700AD

GOLD STANDARD
- This is a standard where all currencies were backed by gold.

The two institutions involved are:
1. **IMF**: To lend money to countries who needed help to keep them from printing more money.
2. **World Bank**: To lend money to the new developing countries that wanted to spend and build up infrastructures.

Currency values are now determined by the FLOATING EXCHANGE SYSTEM which is backed by the demand and supply in the forex market.

CHAPTER 2
MAJOR MARKET PARTICIPANTS

OVERVIEW
- Who are the major market participants?
- What is the role of the central bank in the forex market?
- Who moves the market the most?
- Who moves the market the least?
- What is the role of retail traders?
- Why is it important to know about market participants?

Market participants are the ones that cause the forex market to move. Every trader must know the participants involved in the forex market.
The market participants are as follows:
- The Government
- Central Banks
- Financial Institutions
- Hedgers
- Speculators
- Retail Traders

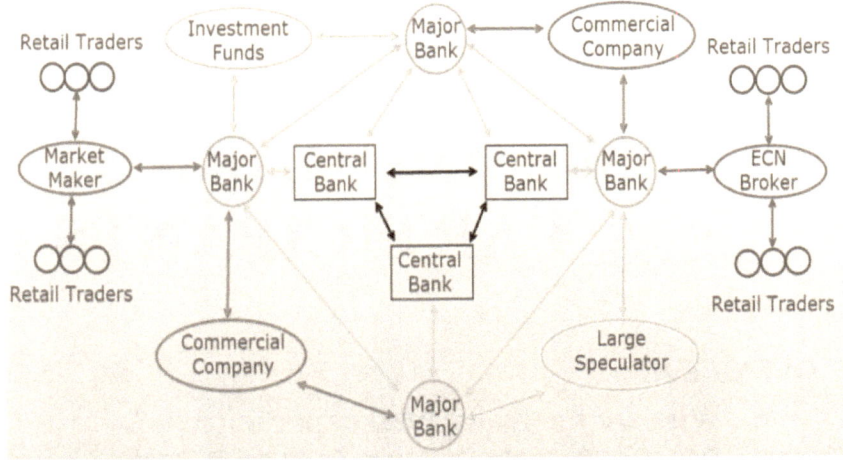

Fig 2.1

CENTRAL BANKS

Central Banks are government organizations that manage their national monetary forms to keep up a solid financial condition, balance exports and imports, avert swelling, and stimulate development inside their economies.

Pay attention to the following news;
1. FOMC
2. Central Bank Rate Decision
3. GDP
4. CPI
5. Unemployment Rate

Central Bank dosen't involve in forex for the profit, but to be able to maintain a healthy economic environment. Fig 2.2 shows the aim of the central bank in the financial market.

Fig 2.2

FINANCIAL INSTITUTIONS

These set of people are one of the major players in the financial market, they involve the large banks, institutional investors, the interbank system. They provide most of the volume that causes the market to move the way it does.

- Major holidays are not the best time to trade
- If there is a major holiday in Japan, then don't trade any of the Japanese yen pairs.

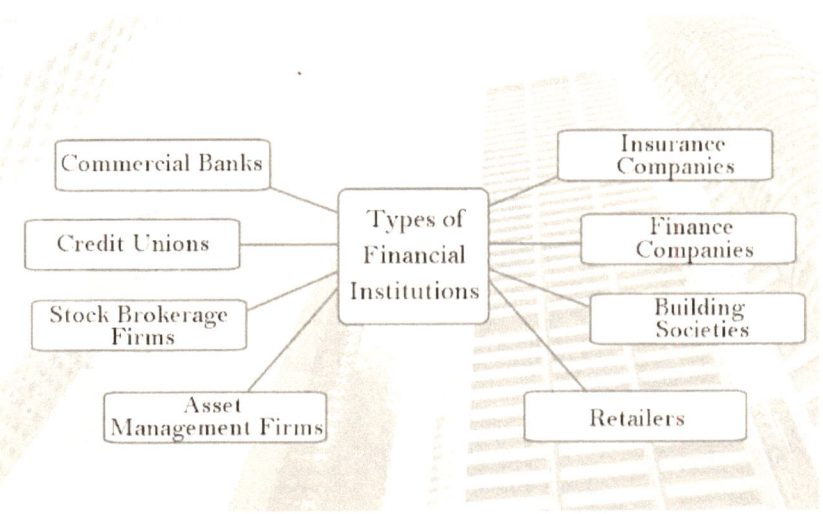

Fig 2.3

- If there is a major holiday in the UK, then don't trade any of the GBP or EUR pairs that day.
- If there is a major holiday in the United State, then don't trade any of the USD pairs.

HEDGERS

These are organizations in an investment position with the intention to protect companies from losses while doing foreign exchange. Their main purpose is helping companies trade.

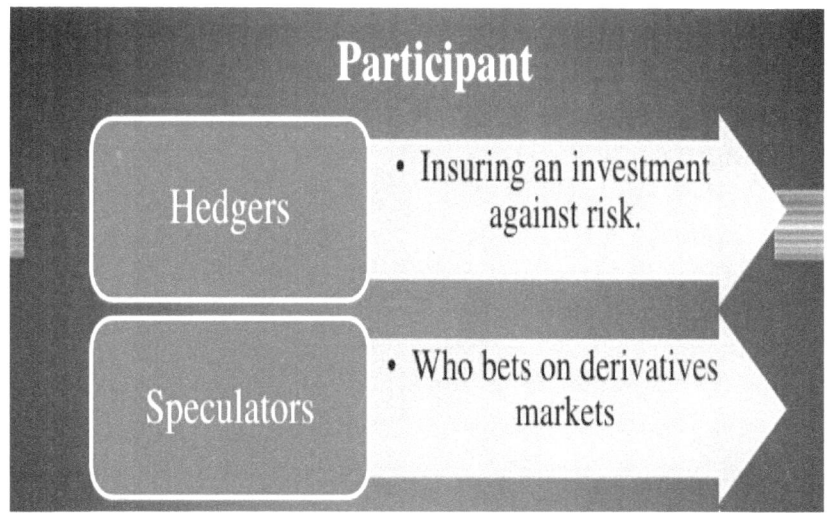

Fig 2.4

SPECULATORS

They are sophisticated risk-taking investors with expertise in the markets in which they are trading.
They attempt to predict price changes in more volatile sections of the market, believing or speculating that a high profit will occur even if the market indicators suggest otherwise.

RETAIL TRADERS

Retail traders are often referred to as individual traders. They buy and sell securities for personal accounts. This is where you and I fall under.
Only 5% of retail traders are successful due to certain knowledge I will be impacting on you in

this book. These are the set of people that move the market the least. And it is advisable they move with the big guys and not go against them to avoid losing money.

CHAPTER 3
WHAT IS FOREX

OVERVIEW
- What is forex?
- What are exchange rates?
- How does supply and demand influence the exchange rate?
- How do we benefit from the foreign exchange market?
- How does the forex market compare to the rest of the market?

Forex is the short form for foreign exchange. It is a global decentralized or over-the-counter market for the trading of currencies. This market decides foreign trade rates for each currency. It includes every aspect of buying, selling and exchanging currencies at current or determined prices.

FOREIGN EXCHANGE RATE
The foreign exchange rate is the rate that buyers pay to exchange their currency. The rate changes due to supply and demand.

EURO CURRENCY EXCHANGE RATES

Currency	Currency Name	Exchange Rate = 1 EUR	Convert
USD	US dollar	1.1095	
JPY	Japanese yen	120.88	
BGN	Bulgarian lev	1.9558	
CZK	Czech koruna	25.543	
DKK	Danish krone	7.4706	

Fig 3.1

From fig 3.1, I used the Euro as a case study; each exchange rate for each currency is the equivalent of one Euro.

When there is a demand for currency, you tend to have a very high exchange rate but when you go to a developing country where there is no much demand, you tend to have a very low exchange rate.

HOW BIG IS THE FOREX MARKET
The foreign exchange market, which is additionally known as "FOREX" is the biggest money related market on the planet. It is worth $5.3 trillion per day in volume which is very large compared to the New York stock exchange that is worth $28 billion per day in volume.

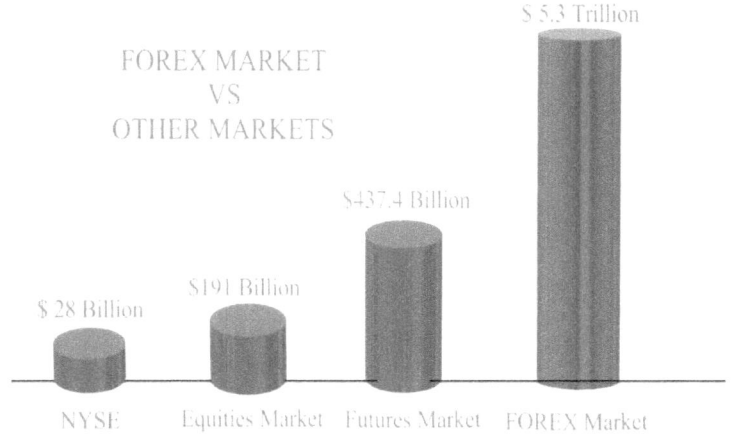

Fig 3.2

The New York stock exchange which is denoted as "NYSE" is the largest stock market in the world, which is followed by the Tokyo stock exchange and then the London stock exchange but all this market is nothing compared to the foreign exchange market. As stocks are being traded in the stock market, currencies are being traded in the foreign exchange market and only a part of this is being traded by the retail traders. I will elaborate more on this in the next chapter.

CHAPTER 4
WHAT IS TRADED IN THE FOREX MARKET

OVERVIEW
- What are currency pairs?
- What are the most common currency pairs?
- What are the major pairs?
- What are minor pairs or cross pairs?
- What is meant by an exotic pair?
- What pairs should I focus on?

The foreign exchange market is all about trading one currency for another. It only has to do with trading currencies and this is done through a broker or dealer. Below you will find the most traded currencies in volume.

MOST TRADED CURRENCIES IN VOLUME
- a) USD   85%
- b) EUR   39%
- c) JPY   19%
- d) GBP   13%
- e) AUD   8%
- f) CHF   6%

g) CAD   5%
h) Others   < 2.5%

Currency Composition of FX Market Turnover (Per Cent)

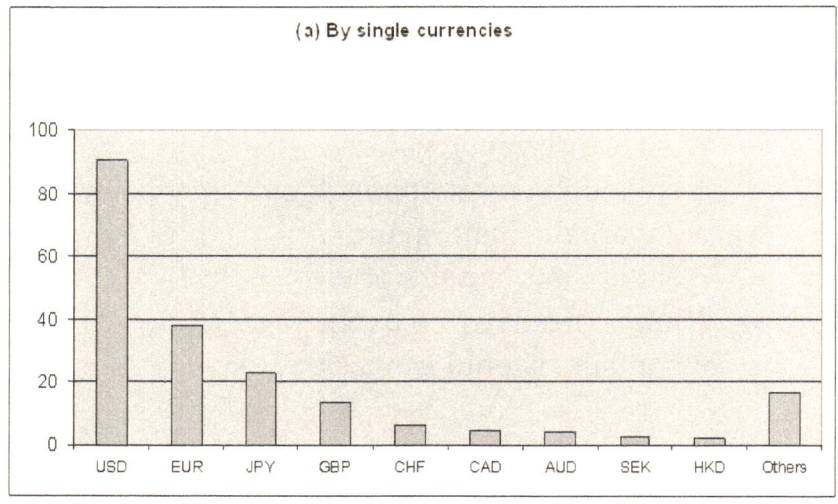

Fig 4.1

All other currencies are <2.5% each. The healthier a country's economy, the better it is for that countries currency. In general, the exchange rate of a currency versus other currencies is a reflection of the condition of that country's economy, compared to other countries' economies.

THINGS THAT AFFECT AN ECONOMY
I. Politics
II. Interest Rates
III. Natural Disasters
IV. Terrorism/Wars
V. Unemployment
VI. Exports/Imports

MAJOR CURRENCIES AND THEIR NICKNAME

SYMBOL	COUNTRY	CURRENCY	NICKNAME
USD	United States	Dollar	Buck
EUR	Euro zone	Euro	Fiber
JPY	Japan	Yen	Yen
GBP	Great Britain	Pound	Cable
CHF	Switzerland	Franc	Swiss
CAD	Canada	Dollar	Loonie
AUD	Australia	Dollar	Aussie
NZD	New Zealand	Dollar	Kiwi

CURRENCY PAIRS

Currency symbols usually have three letters, where the first two letters identify the name of the country and the third letter identifies the name of the country's currency.

Take USD for example, US stands for the United States and D stands for Dollar. JPY, JP stands for Japan and Y stands for YEN.

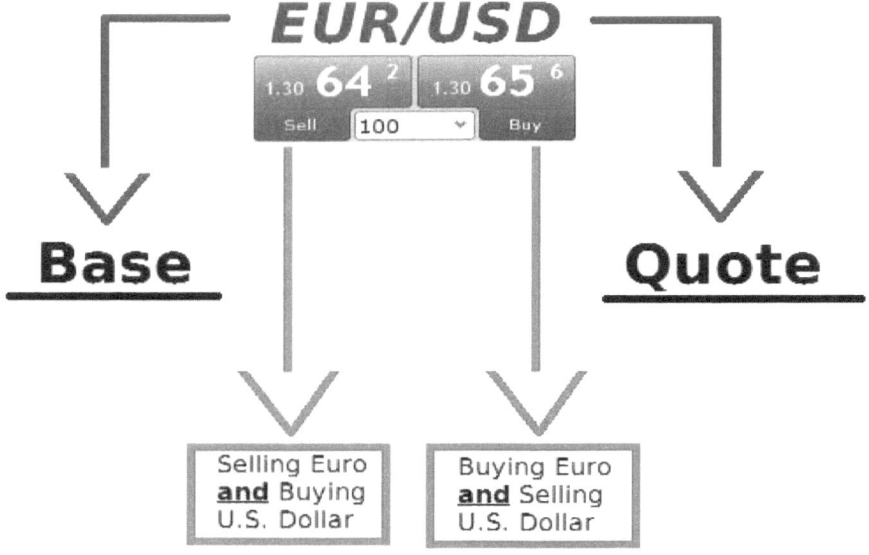

Fig 4.2

BASE CURRENCY

The base currency is the first currency in any currency pair. It shows how much the base currency is worth, as measured against the second currency. For example, if the EURUSD rate is 1.45362, then one Euro is worth 1.45362 US dollar. In the forex markets, the US dollars is normally considered the base currency for quotes, meaning that quotes are expressed as a unit of $1 per the other currency quoted in the pair. The exceptions to this rule are the British pound, Euro and Australian dollar; GBPUSD, EURUSD, AUDUSD, NZDUSD.

QUOTE CURRENCY

The quote currency is the second currency in any currency pair. It is also called the counter currency, For example GBPNZD, EURNZD; NZD is the quote currency in the above pairs.

Since forex trading is a simultaneous buying of one currency and selling of another it is traded in pairs. These pairs are classified as follows;

- Major Currency Pairs
- Major Cross Pairs(Minor currency Pairs)
- Other Cross Pairs
- Exotic Pairs

MAJOR CURRENCY PAIRS

Major currency pairs are pairs that contain the US Dollar or currencies that are paired with the US Dollar. The major pairs are the most liquid and widely traded currency pairs in the world. They are 7 in number.

PAIRS
- EURUSD
- GBPUSD
- USDJPY
- USDCAD
- USDCHF
- AUDUSD
- NZDUSD

COUNTRIES
Euro/United States
UK/US
US/Japan
US/Canada
US/Switzerland
Australia/US
New Zealand/US

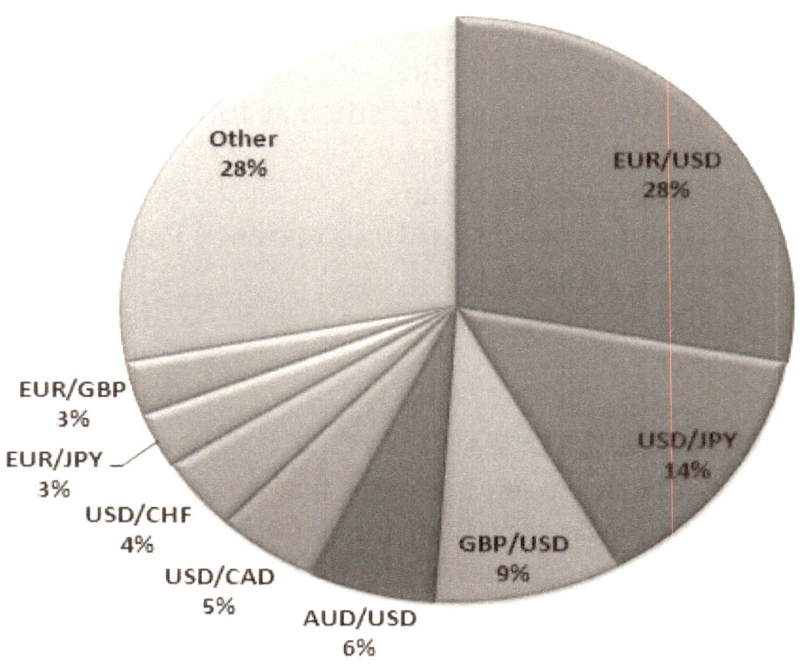

Fig 4.3

MAJOR CROSS PAIRS (MINOR CURRENCY PAIRS)

Any currency pair that does not have the USD is known as crosses or minors and is heavily traded. The most actively traded cross pairs are derived from EUR, JPY, and GBP.

CROSS CURRENCY PAIRS

EUR	JPY	GBP	CAD	AUD	NZD
EUR/GBP	CHF/JPY	GBP/AUD	CAD/CHF	AUD/CHF	NZD/CHF
EUR/CHF	AUD/JPY	GBP/CHF	AUD/CAD	NZD/CHF	
EUR/CAD	GBP/JPY	GBP/CAD	NZD/CAD		
EUR/AUD	CAD/JPY	GBP/NZD			
EUR/NZD	NZD/JPY				
EUR/JPY					

Fig 4.4

YEN CROSSES

EURJPY	Euro/Japan
GBPJPY	UK/Japan
CHFJPY	Switzerland/Japan
CADJPY	Canada/Japan
AUDJPY	Australia/Japan
NZDJPY	New Zealand/Japan

EURO CROSSES

EURCHF	Euro/Switzerland
EURGBP	Euro/UK
EURCAD	Euro/Canada
EURAUD	Euro/Australia
EURNZD	Euro/New Zealand

POUND CROSSES

GBPCHF	UK/Switzerland
GBPAUD	UK/Australia
GBPCAD	UK/Canada
GBPNZD	UK/New Zealand

OTHER CROSSES

AUDCHF	Australia/Switzerland
AUDCAD	Australia/Canada
AUDNZD	Australia/New Zealand
CADCHF	Canada/Switzerland
NZDCHF	NewZealand/Switzerland
NZDCAD	New Zealand/Canada

EXOTIC PAIRS

These are currency pairs that involve a major currency being paired with an emerging economy. These pairs are not heavily traded which leads to higher transaction cost. Examples are as follow;

I. South African Rand (ZAR)
II. South Korean Won (KRW)
III. Hong Kong Dollar (HKD)

IV. Singapore Dollar (SGD)
V. Mexican Peso (MXN)
VI. Indian Rupee (INR)
VII. Russian Federation Ruble (RUB) and lots more which would not be mentioned here.

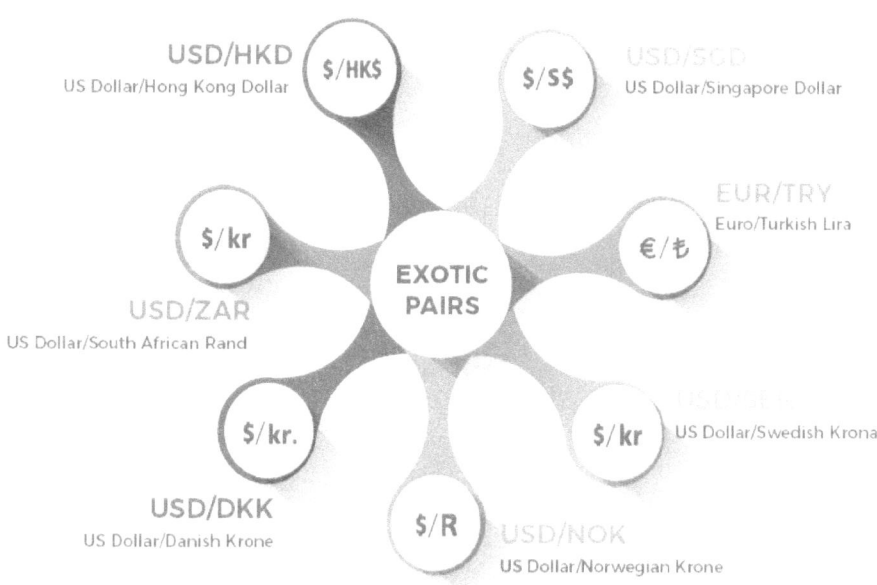

Fig 4.5

The pairs are as follows;
USDZAR	US/South Africa
USDKRW	US/South Korea
USDHKD	US/Hong Kong
USDSGD	US/Singapore

USDMXN   US/Mexico
USDINR   US/India
USDRUB   US/Russia

Depending on the forex broker, you may see the above exotic pairs to trade. Some brokers don't have exotic pairs.

PAIRS YOU SHOULD FOCUS ON

Start with the most common pairs; these are the pairs that are traded frequently in the foreign exchange market and they move the most. These pairs have low transaction costs and have high volume in the market. The pairs include;

- EURUSD
- USDJPY
- GBPUSD
- AUDUSD
- USDCHF
- USDCAD
- EURGBP
- EURJPY
- GBPNZD
- GBPCHF
- GBPCAD

CHAPTER 5
WHEN TO TRADE FOREX

OVERVIEW
- What are the four trading sessions?
- What happens during each trading session?
- When is the best time to trade?
- When is the worst time to trade?
- What do the words; volatility, liquidity, spread, and volume mean in forex?

Trading at the right time can contribute to a trader's success. Before I expatiate more on different trading sessions, I would like to explain some few words;

SPREAD
The contrast between the bid price and the ask price is called spread.
E.g. EURUSD, where EUR is the base currency and USD is the counter currency. When you buy EURUSD that means you are buying EUR and at the same time selling USD.

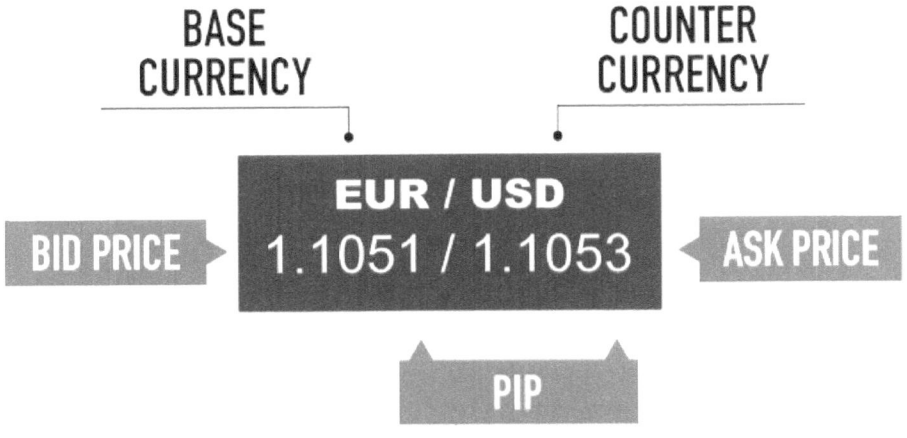

Fig 5.1

All forex quotes consist of two prices which are; Bid price and Ask price. These can be seen on the MT4 platform.

BID PRICE
This is the highest price that a market dealer or broker is willing to pay for goods. As retail traders, this is the price at which you are selling to the market.

ASK PRICE

This is in contrast to bid price; this is the lowest price a prospective seller or broker is willing to accept. This is the price a retail trader is willing to buy from the market.

The contrast between these costs is known as Spread. Let's take EURUSD for example;

XAUUSD 23:54:57 Spread 19	1490.21 Low 1.484.93	1490.40 High 1.494.13
GBPNZD 23:54:57 Spread 181	2.02$68^7$ Low 2.01574	2.02$86^8$ High 2.03400
EURUSD 23:54:57 Spread 13	1.11$70^1$ Low 1.11145	1.11$71^4$ High 1.11706
USDZAR 23:54:57	14.73$60^2$	14.78$46^1$

Fig 5.2

From figure 5.2, EURUSD as an example; the first blue number (1.11701) is the bid price while the second blue number (1.11714) is the ask price. And the spread is seen below the pair which is 13.

PAIR >>> EURUSD

BIDPRICE>>> 1.11701

ASKPRICE>>>1.11714

SPREAD>>>   1.11714
          −
            1.11701
            ‾‾‾‾‾‾‾
            0.00013
            ‾‾‾‾‾‾‾

For USD pairs, the fourth number after the decimal is the pip.

EURUSD has a spread of 1.3 pips.

VOLATILITY

This means when the conditions in the market begin to change rapidly. This is the rate at which the price of a security increases or decreases over a given period. As a retail trader, you will want to trade when there is high volatility and avoid trading when the market has low volatility such as during the Asian session.

HIGH VOLATILITY
1. Big moves take place.
2. Major news releases occur during this period

3. Traders paradise

This is the time to catch the big moves; you see larger candles at this time.

LOW VOLATILITY
   1. Slow sluggish markets.
   2. No major news releases.
   3. Trader's nightmare.

New traders try to force some trades;
Stay out of the market when there is low volatility.

LIQUIDITY

This has to do with the number of participants in the market. This is the degree to which an asset or security can be quickly bought or sold in the market at a price reflecting its intrinsic value. The more the participants in the market at a particular period the higher the liquidity and vice versa.

LOW LIQUIDITY

When there are not too many participants in the market. This is the worst time to trade.

HIGH LIQUIDITY

This is when there are lots of participants in the market. This is the best time to trade. This occurs during the major sessions and the overlaps, traders should look to trade during this period.

VOLUME
This is the size or number of shares that are being traded in the market at a given period. This is simply the amount of currency that changes hands from sellers to buyers.

HIGH VOLUME
This occurs when major market participants are doing a large number of trades in a particular currency.

LOW VOLUME
Not many orders happening. Not many participants are in the market around this time. And this occurs during holidays, the end of the New York session and the beginning of the Sydney session. During this period not very many orders are taken place, so avoid trading during this session.

FOUR MAIN TRADING SESSIONS
1. SYDNEY SESSION
Where the exchanging day authoritatively begins in the forex market. This is the smallest and calmest of the mega-market. This is the Australian market where AUD and NZD move the most. This is not the session to be looking for major moves, as retail traders should avoid this session. This would go a long way in improving your trading success.

This is where the consolidation and manipulation of spread occurs.

The US Session	Overlap	The London Session	The Asian Session
		Liquidity being furnished throughout Europe	Liquidity begins coming in from Wellington, New Zealand
The US session can exhibit behaviors from both the London or Asian Session. The Overlap is often considered 'The Most Liquid Period' of the day		The London session has a proclivity for fast, active moves	The Asian session has a higher tendency for ranges to hold - Support and Resistance to be respected

Fig 5.3

2. TOKYO SESSION

This is the second session. It is the third largest forex trading center in the world. JPY is the third most traded currency in the foreign exchange market which makes it a large one.

During this session, 6% of the foreign exchange transaction occurs. It is a part of the Asian session and has low liquidity and volume with a higher spread. The Asian session comprises of both the Sydney session and Tokyo session.

3. LONDON SESSION

This is the third trading session after the Sydney and Tokyo session. It is the biggest and largest session to trade in. In this session; GBP, EUR, and CHF move the most. This is when you should be looking to trade GBP pairs, EUR pairs, and CHF pairs.

It has historically been the center of trading where 34% of all forex transactions take place. This is the most active session with;
- High Liquidity
- High Volume
- Lower Spreads
- Major News Releases

This is the session you should be looking to trade.

4. NEW YORK SESSION

This session marks the end of the forex day. This is the fourth and the last session for the day, 85% of the trades in this session involve USD pairs. Big moves take place during the early New York session. Major news releases occur during the start of the New York session. In this session USD pairs and CAD pairs move the most. There are high volatility and liquidity in this session but everything dies during the end of the New York session.

THE ABSOLUTE BEST TIME TO TRADE

As a retail trader, you should take note of this, knowing the best time to trade is very important for your success. Please don't joke with this part. You should be looking to trade when there are high volatility and liquidity in the market.

Two major world markets open at the same time which means high volatility, high liquidity, and high volume. The absolute best times to trade are;

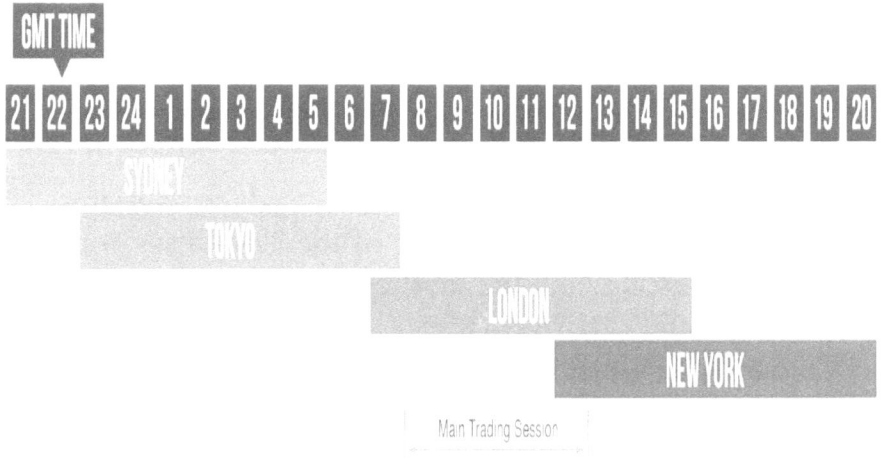

Fig 5.4

- **LONDON/NEW YORK OVERLAP**

This is the most liquid time to trade as two markets are open at the same time. The big guys trade during this period.

- **LONDON/TOKYO OVERLAP**

This is the beginning of the London session, before the end of the Tokyo session; the two big markets usually overlap during this period making the market very volatile. Retail traders should be looking to trade during this period.

WORST TIME TO TRADE

This is the period retail traders should be looking to avoid.

- During the New York session after 6 pm GMT, that is after the London/New York session overlap, during this period the market dies down.
- During the start of the Sydney session through the beginning of the Tokyo session. This is when the market consolidates.
- NON-OVERLAPS
- **MAJOR HOLIDAYS**

In the United States during major holidays, this is not the time to trade any USD pairs as 85% of pairs involve the USD.

In Europe during major holidays being that they are the center of all world trade, this is not a good time to trade.

- **CONSOLIDATION**

This occurs when there are lots of small candlesticks not going in any direction in particular. They have sideways movement overall. This is a trader's nightmare.

CHAPTER 6
BUYING VS SELLING

OVERVIEW
- What is the distinction between buying and selling?
- What does a buy look like?
- What does a sell look like?
- How and why does the market move?

BUY; BULLS; LONG

When you hear the word buy, bull, long, they all mean the same thing.

When currency value is expected to rise, you would want to place a buy. When a market is bullish that means the market is in an uptrend, it is going up.

SELL; BEARS; SHORT

When you hear the word sell, bear, or short, it is simply saying the same thing.

At the point when currency worth is required to fall, you would need to put a sell. When a market is bearish, that means the market is in a downtrend, it is going down.

WHAT HAPPENS WHEN YOU PLACE AN ORDER

I. Buyers in the market cause exchange rate value to increase due to an increase in demand for the currency.
II. Sellers in the market cause exchange rate value to decrease due to low demand for that currency.

The market movement happens due to demand and supply.

Fig 6.1

THE POWERFUL PHRASES

- Overbought ⟹ Best time to sell
- Oversold ⟹ Best time to buy

When a price has gone up for too long it tends to be overbought and would sell off. When a price has gone down for too long it tends to be oversold and would start to buy at that point.

This doesn't happen every time, cases when it doesn't happen, is when the price is in a strong uptrend or downtrend which can cause the market to get stuck in the overbought or oversold for an extended period.

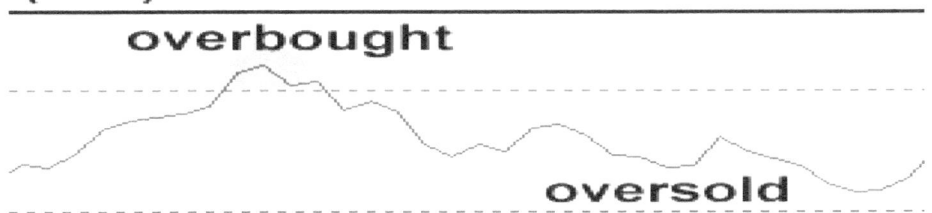

Fig 6.2

NOTE: The trend is your friend; you do not want to go against the trend.

NOTE: When an exchange rate is low, you would want to place a buy order (Buy low) and when the exchange rate is high, you would want to place a sell order (Sell high).

PART 2
TRADING TERMS

CHAPTER 7
WHAT ARE PIPS AND HOW THEY ARE CALCULATED

OVERVIEW
- What is a pip?
- How do you ascertain what number of pips the market moved?

PIP

This is the unit of measurement to express the change in value in the market. You will often hear the word "pips", like how length is measured in meter and temperature is measured in degree that's how the movement in the foreign exchange market is measured in pips.

The pip is the fourth number after the decimal for USD pairs. In this chapter, I would be showing you how to calculate pips for different pairs.

HOW TO CALCULATE PIPS (USD PAIRS)
This is basically for USD pairs

EXAMPLE: You enter NZDUSD at 4.56567 and exit at 4.56772 for a buy. How many pips is this?

SOLUTION

Entry price ⟹ 4.56567
Take profit ⟹ 4.56772

⟹ $\quad\begin{array}{r} 4.56772 \\ -\ 4.56567 \\ \hline 0.00205 \end{array}$

NOTE: For USD pairs, the pip is the fourth digit after your decimal point. Every retail trader should know this. Since it is the fourth number, we divide our value by 0.0001(four places after the decimal).

⟹ $\dfrac{0.00205}{0.0001} = 20.5 \text{ pips}$

We divide our value by 0.0001 or alternatively move the decimal by four places as the pip is the fourth number after the decimal.

PIPETTE

This is the fifth number after the decimal.

1.3020¹0

The number in the circle (1) is the pipette, this is the way it is seen on most trading platform like Mt4, trading view.

What is a Pip in Forex Trading?

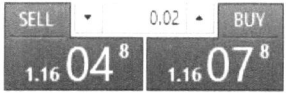

Currency Pair	Pip	Pipette or Point
EURUSD	1.16048/1.16078	1.16048/1.16078
EURJPY	124.663/124.678	124.663/124.678

How to Calculate Pips Profit?

Fig 7.1

EXAMPLE 2: You enter NZDUSD at 1.09892 and exit at 1.16971 for a buy. How many pips?

SOLUTION

Entry Price $\implies$ 1.09892
Take Profit $\implies$ 1.16971

$\implies$ $\quad\begin{array}{r} 1.16971 \\ -\underline{1.09892} \\ \underline{0.07079} \end{array}$

For USD pairs, since the pip is the fourth digit after the decimal, we divide by 0.0001.

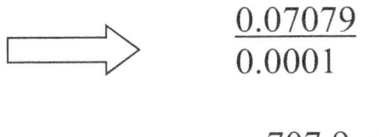

$$\frac{0.07079}{0.0001}$$

$= 707.9$ pips

Alternatively, move the decimal by four places since pip is the fourth value. This should be easier than the first step.
After subtracting, we have

$$0.07079$$

Moving by four decimal places, we have
707.9 pips

HOW TO CALCULATE STOP LOSS AND TAKE PROFIT FROM ENTRY PRICE

This section is very important, some retail traders still find it hard to get a pip target for their stop loss or take profit from their entry price.

EXAMPLE 1: You enter EURUSD at 1.20540 for a buy with a take profit of 50pips and stop loss of 20pips.
What are your take profit and your stop loss?

SOLUTION

Entry price ⟹ 1.20540
Profit target ⟹ 50 pips
Loss target ⟹ 20 pips

Take profit ⟹ 50 × 0.0001

=0.005

Take profit ⟹ 1.20540 + 0.005

=1.21040

NOTE: Value must be five digits after the decimal 1.2104 is the same as 1.21040

NOTE: We used 0.0001 to multiply because pip is the fourth digit after the decimal.

NOTE: When you are given an entry price, a profit target, and a stop-loss target, you divide by 0.0001 to get the pip difference between the prices. When given an entry price and a certain pip target, you multiply by 0.0001 to get your take profit and stop-loss as shown in the above examples.

Stop-loss ⟹ 20 × 0.0001

=0.002

Since it is stop loss, the value will be subtracted

Stop-loss ⟹ 1.20540 − 0.002

=1.20340

NOTE: The following should be noted

- When you buy a currency, you add the calculated value to entry price to get your take profit and subtract to get your stop loss.
- When you sell a currency, you subtract the calculated value to get your take profit and add to get your stop loss.
- When you want to calculate the number of pips between an entry price and take profit or stop loss, subtract the smaller from the bigger.

EXAMPLE: You sold USDCAD at 1.03452 and have a profit target of 80 pips and a stop-loss target of 30 pips. What are the take profit and stop-loss?

SOLUTION

Entry price ⟹ 1.03452
Profit target ⟹ 80 pips
Loss target ⟹ 30 pips

Take profit ⟹ 80 × 0.0001

$$=0.008$$

Take profit = 1.03452 − 0.008 (Since it is a sell)

$$=1.02652$$

Stop-loss ⟹ 30 × 0.0001

= 0.003

Stop-loss = 1.03452 + 0.003

= 1.03752

JPY PAIRS

These pairs are calculated differently from USD pairs. The pip is usually the second number after the decimal.

EXAMPLE: 112.230

The circled number is the pipette, while the second number after the decimal is the pip.

HOW TO CALCULATE PIPS OF JPY PAIRS

Entry price = 112.231
Take profit = 112.456

Is this a buy or sell?

⟹ 112.456
− 112.231
   0.225

Since the pip is the second number after the decimal, we divide by 0.01, unlike USD pairs.

$$\Longrightarrow \quad 0.225 \div 0.01$$

$$= 22.5 \text{ pips}$$

Alternatively, since the pip is the second number after the decimal we move by two places

$$0.\underset{\smile\smile}{225}$$

=22.5 pips

Example 2: Entry price = 112.231
Take profit =119.560

$$\Longrightarrow \quad \begin{array}{r} 119.560 \\ -112.231 \\ \hline 7.329 \end{array}$$

7.329 ÷ 0.01 = 732.9 pips

HOW TO GET YOUR TAKE PROFIT OR STOP LOSS FROM YOUR ENTRY PRICE FOR JPY PAIRS

EXAMPLE: You bought USDJPY at 112.231 with a take profit target of 50 pips and a tight stop-loss of 15 pips. What are your take profit price and your stop-loss price?

SOLUTION

Entry price = 112.231

For profit target of 50 pips

$$= 50 \times 0.01$$

(Since the pip is the second number after the decimal for JPY pairs)

$$= 0.5$$

Take profit = 112.231 + 0.5
Take profit = 112.731

For stop-loss target of 15 pips

$$= 15 \times 0.01$$

$$= 0.15$$

Stop loss = 112.231 − 0.15

$$= 112.081$$

GOLD PAIRS (XAU XXX)

The pip is usually the first number after the decimal for a gold pair.

$$1221.12$$

2 is the pipette, while the number after the decimal is the pip.

HOW TO CALCULATE PIPS FOR XAU PAIRS

Entry price ⟹ 1221.12

Take profit ⟹ 1298.32

$$\begin{array}{r} 1298.32 \\ -1221.12 \\ \hline 77.20 \end{array}$$

Since for gold pairs, pip is the first number after the decimal we divide by 0.1

$$77.20 \div 0.1$$

$$= 772 \text{ pips}$$

Is this a buy or sell?

HOW TO GET YOUR TAKE PROFIT OR STOP LOSS FROM ENTRY PRICE

You have an entry price on XAUUSD at 1221.12 to take a profit of over 772 pips. What is the take profit price?

SOLUTION

For take profit of 772 pips, we multiply by 0.1

$$772 \times 0.1$$
$$= 77.2$$

Adding the calculated value to the entry price will give us the take profit price

$$= 1221.12 + 77.2$$

Take profit price = 1298.32

CHAPTER 8
WHAT ARE LEVERAGE AND LOTS

OVERVIEW
- What are lots?
- What are all the lot sizes?
- How do lots correlate to profit or loss?
- What is leverage?
- How does leverage benefit me?
- How does leverage hurt me?

LOTS

These refer to a contract being made of a certain size. They are purchased in bundles of units called <u>lots</u>.

There are standardized contract sizes;

Lot Size		Units
Standard Lot	⟹	100,000
Mini Lot	⟹	10,000
Micro Lot	⟹	1,000
Nano Lot	⟹	100

LOT SIZE	VOLUME	$/PIP
Standard Lot	1.00	$10/pip
Mini Lot	0.10	$1/pip
Micro Lot	0.01	$0.10/pip

LEVERAGE

Leverage is a technique that uses borrowed capital to build potential future returns.

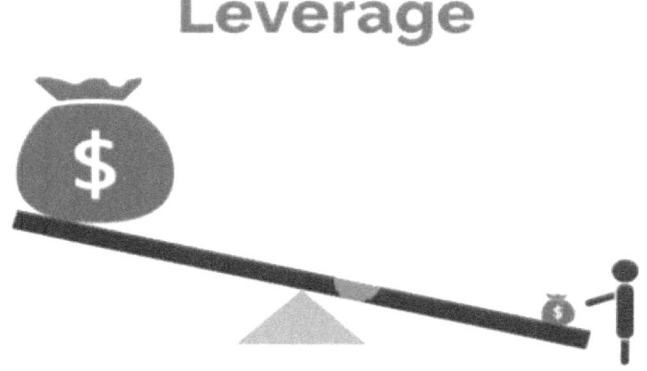

Fig 8.2

LEVERAGE EXAMPLE

1:200 Leverage ⟹ For every $1 in your account, your broker lets you leverage $200.

That means if you have an account balance of $1000 and you use a leverage of 1:200, you can take a trade worth of $200,000. The same goes for a leverage of 1:100; you would be able to take trade worth of $100,000.

True leverage is what you use at any given time. Don't be so fast in using high leverage because the higher the leverage, the higher your chances of losing money.

HOW TO CALCULATE LOT SIZE AND LEVERAGE

The risk percentage is the most important thing in forex. And it depends on your risk and leverage.

$$\$ \text{ Risk} = \% \text{ Risk} \times \frac{\text{Account equity}}{100}$$

$$\text{Lot Size} = \frac{\$ \text{ Risk}}{\text{Pip value} \times \text{SL}}$$

Pip value depends on the leverage of your account; $Risk and %Risk does not depend on the leverage at all.

HOW TO CALCULATE LOT SIZE

The easiest way to do this is as follows;
- Search for "position size calculator" on Google
- Select the first result which is (www.myfxbook.com)
- Then input the following, don't forget to risk not more than 3% of your account.

    (1) Account base currency, what your account is denominated in
    (2) Account size, this is your account balance
    (3) Risk ratio, percentage of your account you are willing to lose which should not be more than 3%
    (4) Stop loss, This is your stop loss target in pips
    (5) Currency pair, This is the currency pair you want to trade
    (6) Then finally you click on calculate, and boom everything is done automatically for you.

CHAPTER 9
YOUR TRADING WINDOW

OVERVIEW
- What does balance mean?
- What does equity mean?
- What does margin mean?
- What does free margin mean?
- What does margin level percentage mean?
- What is a stop out level?

BALANCE

This is the amount of money you have when there are no open positions, the total money that is available for withdrawal.

EQUITY

Equity is your balance plus floating profit/loss of your open position. When there is no open position and no floating profit/loss, then equity is equal to the account balance.

MARGIN

Margin is the amount of money that is locked when the position is open and is added back to the account balance when the position is closed. The money that gets involved in a trade or position acts as collateral.

	372.60 USD	+
Balance:		100 000.00
Equity:		100 372.60
Margin:		1 116.60
Free Margin:		99 256.00
Margin Level (%):		8 989.13
Positions		
EURUSD, buy 0.50 1.11660 → 1.12034		**187.00**
EURUSD, buy 0.50 1.11660 → 1.12034		**187.00**

Fig 9.1

FREE MARGIN

This is Equity minus Margin. It is the available money for withdrawal when on position. When there is no position, the free margin will be equal to equity and total balance.

$$\text{Free Margin} = \text{Equity} - \text{Margin}$$

MARGIN LEVEL %

This is the ratio of Equity to Margin.

$$\frac{\text{Equity}}{\text{Margin}} \times 100\%$$

This is very important as it is used to determine if a trader can take any new position when they already have some positions. When the margin level reaches 100%, you may not want to take on any new position as the limit is 100% with most brokers. When the equity equals margin, margin level reaches 100%; this occurs when the market goes against you, as a result, account equity equals margin and your margin level reaches 100%, the broker will close the biggest losing position.

STOP OUT LEVEL

This is the level when a broker starts closing losing positions automatically if your margin level reaches 5% (Depends on the broker), it starts to close from the biggest losing position first, thereby increasing the margin level. As the positions are closed automatically, the margin level increases.

CANCELED BY THE DEALER

This occurs when you have some open positions and some pending orders at the same time, then the market reaches where one of your pending orders are placed while you don't have enough free margin in your account. The pending order will not trigger or will be canceled automatically due to insufficient free margin.

CHAPTER 10
TYPES OF ORDERS

OVERVIEW
- What is market execution order?
- What is the difference between limit orders and stop orders?
- What is a stop order?
- What is a limit order?
- How do you place a pending order?

The term order refers to how you would want to enter or exit the market. Here we would discuss the different types of forex orders that can be placed in the forex market. There are two types of orders in the foreign exchange market; which are the Market execution order and the Pending order. The pending order is further divided into four, which are sell stop, buy stop, sell limit, and buy limit.

MARKET EXECUTION
Market execution is a type of order where the trader agrees to buy/sell a particular currency at any price that is currently available. In other words, it means buying/selling a currency at that

particular time. The broker puts you in the market immediately either for a buy or sell.

PENDING ORDER

Pending order is a request made by a trader to the broker to say at which price a position should be opened or closed for a particular currency. Using pending orders allows a trader to make profit when there is no opportunity to watch the charts. There are four types of pending order.

STOP ORDERS

Stop orders are orders that are triggered when the market moves past a specific price point. A threshold has to be crossed only once before you are entered into the trade. Once the price is crossed, the stop order becomes a market order.

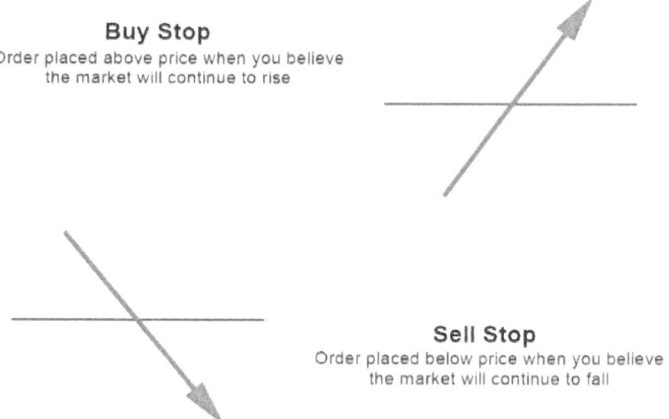

Fig 10.1

SELL STOPS

A sell stop order is entered at a stop price that is below the current market price expecting the price to drop. When the threshold is crossed, you are entered into the trade.

BUY STOPS

A buy stop order is entered at a stop price that is above the current market price expecting the price to continue to move up. When the threshold is crossed, you are entered into the trade for a buy.

LIMIT ORDERS

A limit order is a type of order to buy/sell a particular currency at a specified price. A threshold has to be crossed before you are entered into the trade and expecting it to turn around.

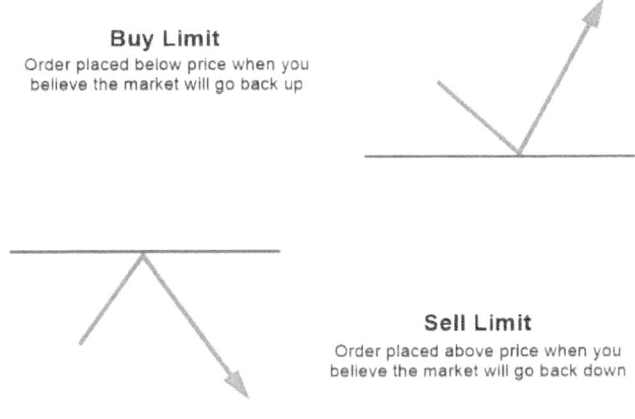

Buy Limit
Order placed below price when you believe the market will go back up

Sell Limit
Order placed above price when you believe the market will go back down

Fig 10.2

SELL LIMIT

Sell limit is a sell pending order that is placed above market price expecting it to turn around and fall. After entering your sell limit, the market must climb higher before it turns around and fall.

BUY LIMIT

A buy limit order is an order to buy/sell an asset below market price expecting price to turn around and move up. After entering your buy limit, the market must drop before it turns around for a buy.

STOP LOSS AND TAKE PROFIT

STOP LOSS

A stop loss is a function offered by brokers to limit losses in volatile markets moving in contrary to the initial trade you took. If a trade goes the wrong direction, stop loss will stop the order with your losses. Always put a stop loss because this is your account's safety.

TAKE PROFIT

Take profit request is a request that closes your trade once it reaches a certain level of profit. When your take profit request is hit on a trade, the trade is closed at the current market value. It prevents the price from reaching your desired target and then turning around. Once price reaches this price, you are been taken out of the market.

Fig 10.3

From figure 10.3,
- *When in a buy market, stop loss is placed below the entry price and take profit is placed above the entry price.*
- *When in a sell market, stop loss is placed above the entry price and take profit is placed below the entry price.*

PART 3
ANALYZING THE FOREX MARKET

CHAPTER 11
THREE TYPES OF ANALYSIS

OVERVIEW
- What are the three types of analysis?
- How are they different?
- Which is the best to use?

There are three basic types of forex market analysis; Fundamental, technical and sentiment analysis. It is up to the individual trader to try and find out what type of analysis suits their trading style.

TECHNICAL ANALYSIS
Technical analysis is a type of analysis that is used by traders to study price movements. This is based on historical price movements to determine where a given currency is headed.

Traders study historical price movements to determine where the price could go.

Technical analyst uses;
    1. Charts

2. Indicators
3. Price patterns
4. Price action

FUNDAMENTAL ANALYSIS

Fundamental analysis is often used to analyze changes in the forex market by monitoring figures such as interest rates, unemployment rates, gross domestic product (GDP), and other types of economic data that come out of countries. This type of analysis includes political, social, and economic news to gauge how the market will do along with a countries potential economic outlook.

If a certain country does well then its currency should do well. Fundamental analysis is not enough for success but it is very helpful.

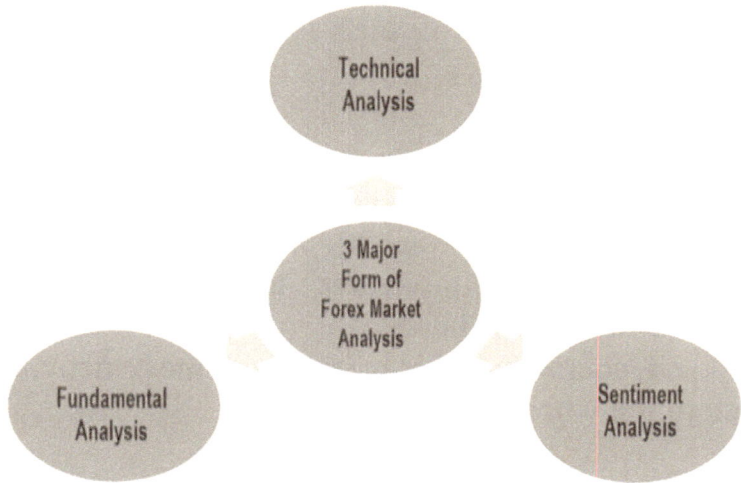

Fig 11.1

TOOLS TO STUDY FUNDAMENTAL

I. Check out Bloomberg.com
II. Check out Bloomberg.tv
III. Forex factory
IV. Various economic calendars

SENTIMENTAL ANALYSIS

Sentimental analysis has to do with the overall feeling of the market. This analysis is not as important to understand every detail of news, but more important to gauge how people are responding to the news and how that shows up in the market. Sentimental analysis is very important and can be used alongside technical analysis. In this analysis, every trader has his or her own opinion of why the is acting the way it does and whether to trade in the same direction as the market or against it.

WHICH TYPE OF ANALYSIS FOR FOREX TRADING IS THE BEST

There is no best; they are all just different ways to look at the market. Do not be fooled by this one-sided extremist. The three analysis works best when used together; the fundamental factor shapes the sentiment, while technical analysis helps us to visualize that sentiment and apply a framework to create our trading plan.

In this book, I will mainly be discussing further on technical analysis and how they can be best applied.

CHAPTER 12
WHAT IS A TREND

OVERVIEW
- What is a trend?
- How can you ascertain if the market is trending?

In the financial markets, there is an articulation: 'the trend is your friend'; and keeping in mind that this expression may bode well, by and by it is as hazy as it can get. Be that as it may, what is a trend and how would we characterize it just as trade with it?

TREND DEFINITION
By definition, a trend is a general direction in which market value or price of a currency evolves. Trends can be upwards (bullish market), downwards (bearish market) or sideways (ranging market). There is no specific timeline for a direction to be considered a trend, but overall, the longer the direction is sustained, the more qualified the trend becomes.

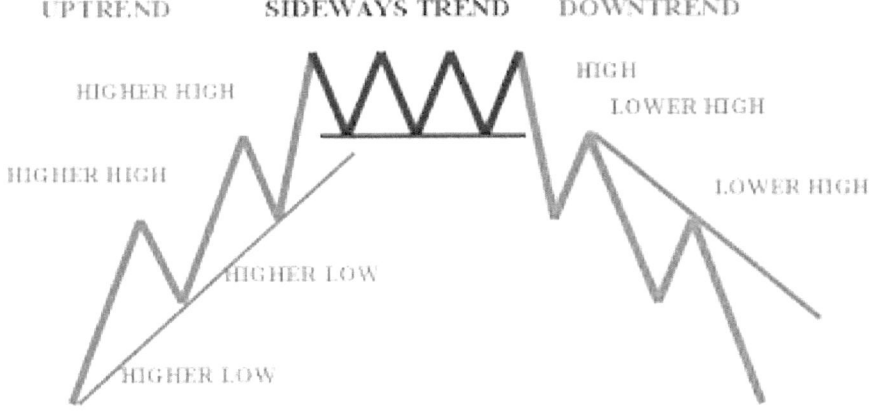

Fig 12.1

TYPES OF TREND

When it comes to the foreign exchange market, price moves in three ways. Either price is going up, going down, or it is moving sideways.

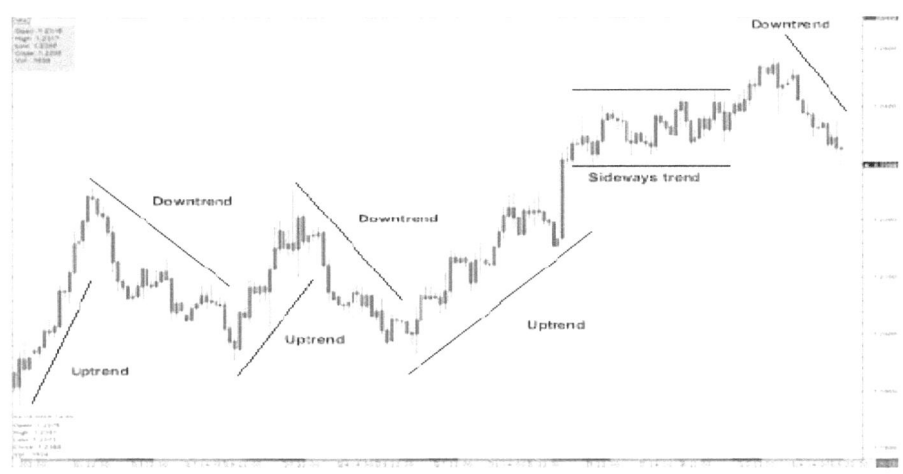

Fig 12.2

1. UPTREND

When a price is said to be in an uptrend, it will consist of higher highs and higher lows. This is an upward tendency or rise in the value of a currency or asset. What characterizes an uptrend market are higher highs and higher lows. When trading in an uptrend market, you would look for **long term buys** and **short term sells**. Figure 12.3 is a perfect uptrend with higher highs and higher lows.

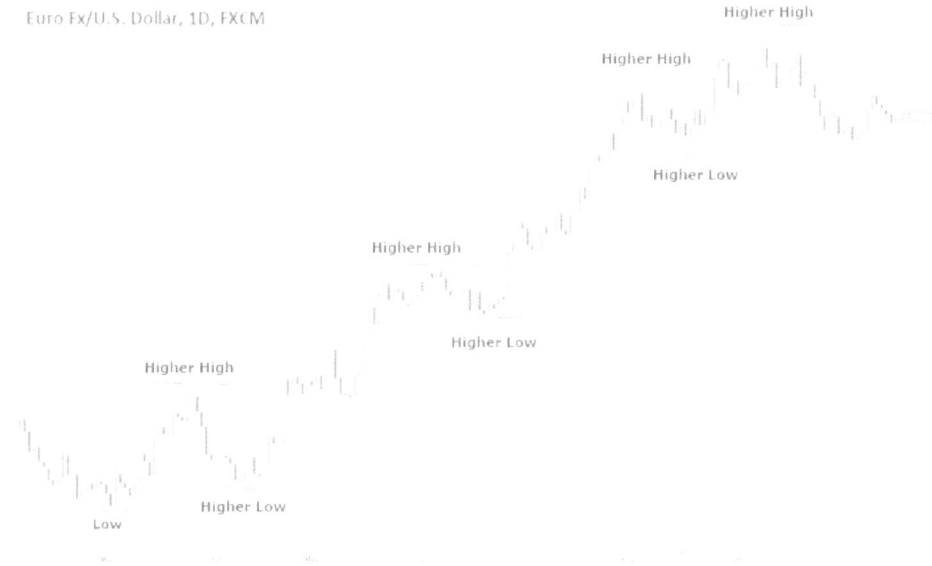

Fig 12.3

RETRACEMENT

This is when the market goes in the opposite direction of the overall direction for a short period. This is also known as **Pullback**.

When you miss an opportunity for a buy in an uptrend, do not rush to enter the market instead wait for pullback or retracement before going in. This is what professionals do. If the price doesn't pull back then there is no need to enter the market because the first rule in trading is (Protect the money).

Fig 12.4

2. DOWNTREND

When a price is said to be in a downtrend, it will comprise of lower highs and lower lows. This is the tendency of price to consistently move downwards with little upwards movement. The push downwards can be caused by fundamentals,

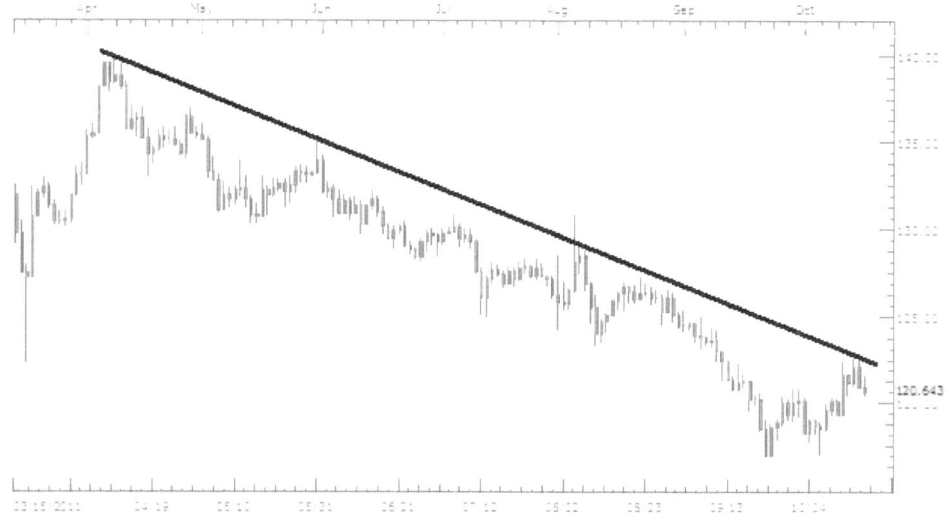

Fig 12.5

This is why all forex analysis is important. When trading in a downtrend market, you would look for **long term sells** and **short term buys**. It is best to find the trend on a higher timeframe.

Fig 12.6

3. RANGING MARKET

This type of market is also known as **consolidation**. This is the sideways movement of price; it consistently oscillates between fixed levels of support (bottom) and resistance (top). During this period no higher/lower highs or lows are being formed. The market is moving sideways due to indecision. This is the period you will want to stay out of the market because the market has no direction. It usually occurs during the Asian session and the end of the New York session. As a trader who wants to consistently make profit, you should avoid trading when there is consolidation in the market.

Fig 12.7

NOTE: The trending market is the best market to trade on because it cuts your risk.

IDENTIFYING A TREND
The simplest method to recognize trends is by watching the raw price action of an asset. Price action (technical) traders believe that the information provided by a candlestick is sufficient to decipher the market. After all, they say 'candles exhaust themselves to give light to men'.

An uptrend is identified when an asset's price is consistently making higher highs and lows, while a downtrend occurs when the price is making lower lows and lower highs.

I. USING PRICE ACTION TO IDENTIFY A TREND
Trending markets (uptrend and downtrend) are ideal for swing traders who can set wide price targets, whereas ranging markets are suitable for scalpers and day traders who seek quick profits by setting short price targets. To select an ideal entry and exit points in a trend, price action traders use trend lines and channels.

In an uptrend, a trend line is drawn from one particular swing low, connecting it to another successive but higher swing low and projecting the line into the future. The line then acts as a diagonal support line, with optimal buy position entry points identified when price touches or comes closer to the trend line.

The reverse also applies on a downtrend, when a trend line is drawn from one particular swing high, connecting it to another successive but lower swing high, and projecting the line into the future. The trend line then acts as a diagonal resistance line, with optimal sell position entry points identified when the price touches or comes close to the line.

Fig 12.8

In a range- bound market, the trend lines are drawn as horizontal lines along clearly defined areas of support and resistance. Traders will then seek to place buy orders when the price is at or close to the support line and sell orders when the price is at or near the resistance line.

II. USING MOVING AVERAGES

Moving averages are the oldest and undoubtedly the most popular technical analysis tool available. They not only help in establishing a trend direction but also trend momentum and possible trend reversals. The computation of moving averages allows them to smooth out price action empowering one to effortlessly decide the trend direction. When prices sustain above a moving average, it simply implies a confirmed uptrend is in place. Traders may infer a trend's momentum by observing the slope of the moving average. That is, a steeper slope implies a more momentous trend and vice versa.

To perform much further analysis, traders combine different moving averages. In this way, they can confirm prevailing trends as well as spot potential trend reversals early enough. When the faster moving average is above the slower one, an uptrend is confirmed; and when the faster moving average is below the slower one, a downtrend is confirmed. Trend reversals are foreseen when a moving average cross over occurs. For instance, if prices are trending higher, and the shorter period (faster) moving average crosses the longer period (slower) moving average downwards; this signals that the uptrend may soon reverse.

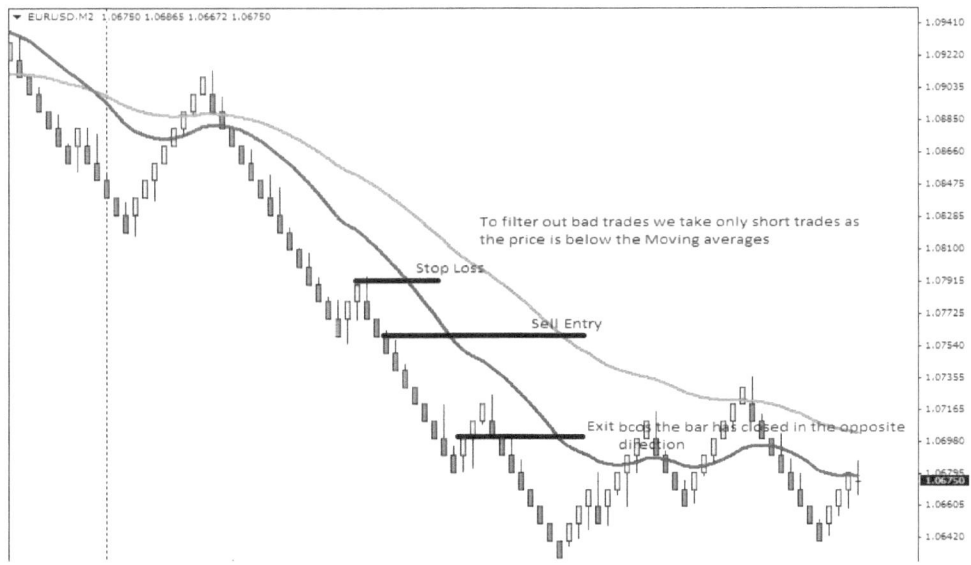

Fig 12.9

Channels are essentially parallel trend lines drawn in a manner to ensure the price action is contained within the trend line borders. Channels are ideal for placing targets; for instance, in an uptrend, the upper line represents areas where the price may begin to retrace or decline, and this would be a good level to exit a buy order.

CHAPTER 13
WHAT IS PRICE ACTION

OVERVIEW
- What are candlesticks?
- How do you read candlesticks?
- How can you use candlesticks to help you trade?

WHAT IS PRICE ACTION?

Price action is the movement of an asset price over time. Price action forms the basis for all technical analysis of a stock, commodity or currency. These involve chart pattern, candlestick pattern, support and resistance, trend line and so on. Price action is what is being used by technical traders, most time they ignore the fundamentals. I would emphasize more on this in my next chapter.

WHAT IS CANDLESTICK?

A candlestick is a type of price chart used that displays the high, low, open, and closing prices of security (commodity, currency, etc.) for a specific period. It started from the Japanese rice vendors and merchants to track market costs and day by day energy many years ago before turning out to be advanced in the United States.

The wide piece of the candle is known as the "genuine body" and tells financial specialists whether the end price was higher or lower than the opening price. The candlestick's shadow shows the day's high and low and how they compare to the open and close. A candlestick's shape varies based on the relationship between the day's high, low, opening and closing prices.

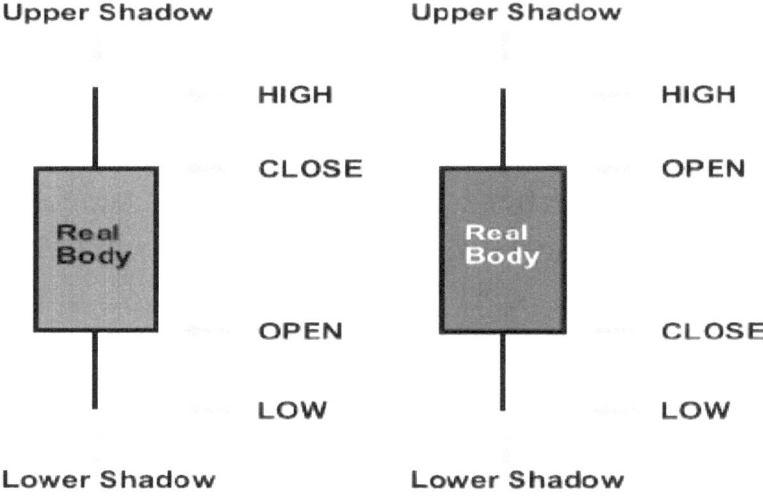

Fig 13.1

Candlesticks mirror the effect of financial specialist's sentiment on security prices and are utilized by technical analysts to determine when to enter and exit trades. Candlestick charting depends on a method created in Japan during the 1700s for tracking the cost of rice. Candlesticks are an appropriate system for trading any liquid financial resource such as stocks, foreign exchange, and futures.

WICKS TELL YOU A LOT ABOUT DECISIONS BEING MADE IN THE BACKGROUND

Pay attention to all the wicks, they tell you a lot. It might be that the market is about to do a major

Fig 13.2

reversal or take the opposite direction.

Wicks are one of the confirmations you see to know the direction the market wants to go.

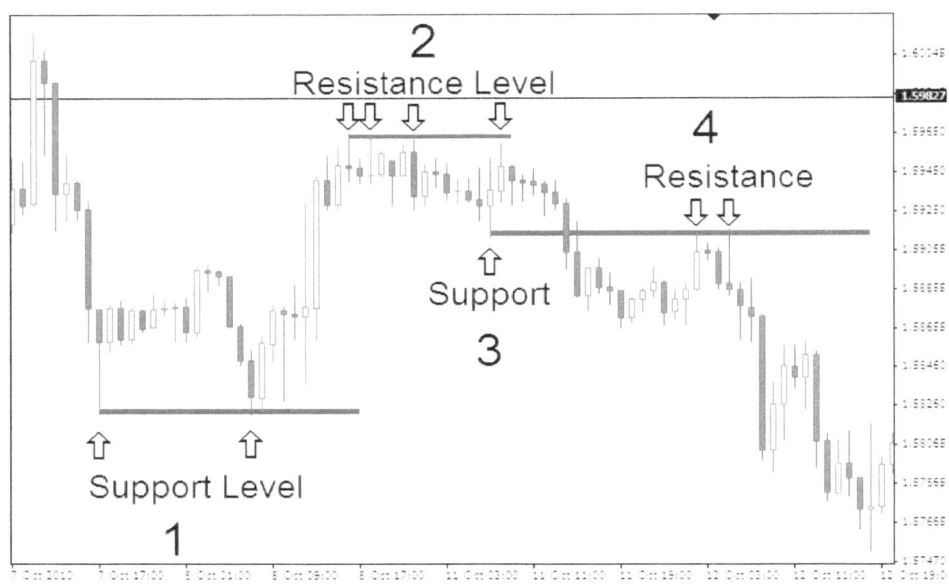

Fig 13.3

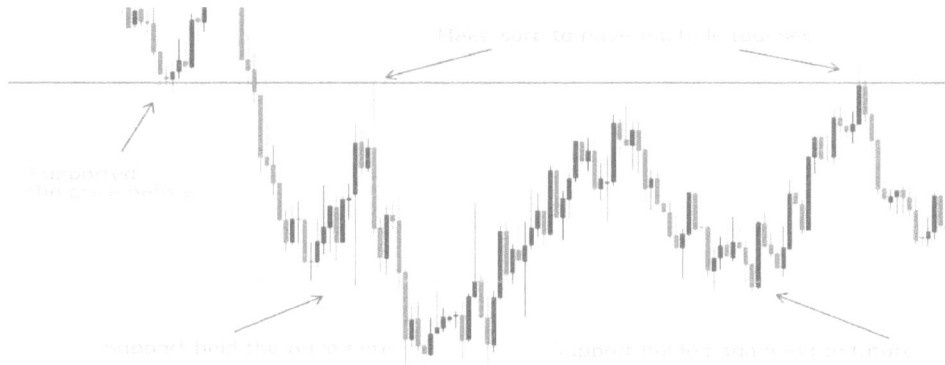

Fig 13.4

CHAPTER 14
SUPPORT, RESISTANCE AND TRENDLINES

OVERVIEW

- What is support?
- What is resistance?
- How do you draw support and resistance?

RESISTANCE LINE

The resistance line acts as a ceiling; this is where price struggles to break above it. Sometimes it doesn't just act as a line, it acts as a zone. This illustration is shown in figure 14.1

SUPPORT LINE

Support is what acts as a floor. Price is supported in this area; it is held up in this area and struggles to break below it.

NOTE: The more touches, the stronger that area becomes.

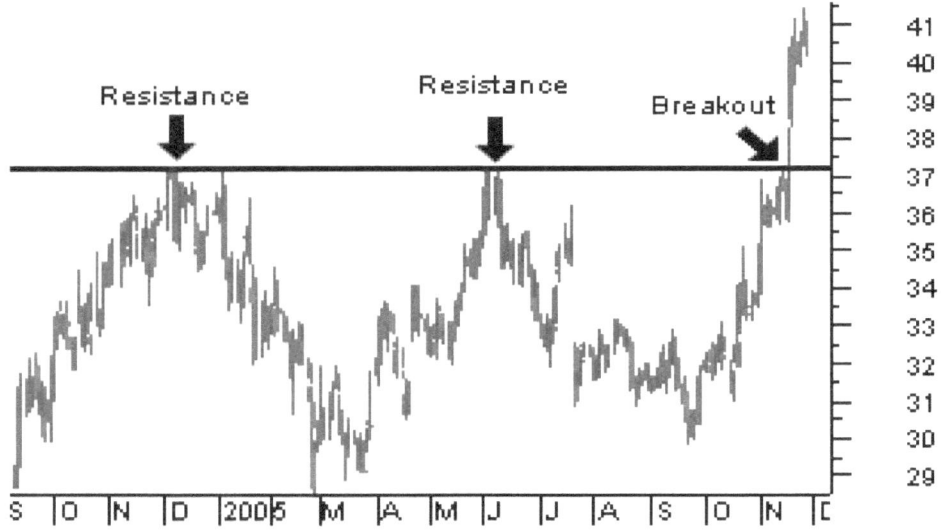

Fig 14.1

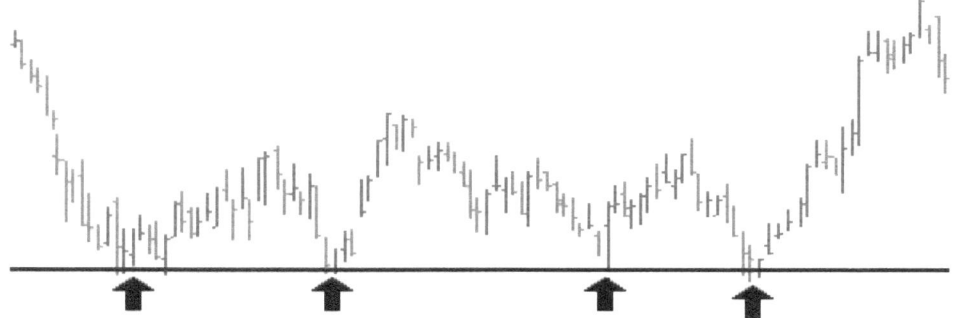

Fig 14.2

When drawing your support and resistance, look for zones that have more touches, then you draw your lines. It doesn't need to be a line; they are more like zones or areas.

HOW TO DRAW SUPPORT AND RESISTANCE

1. To draw your support and resistance, you see it as an area, not a line.
2. Change your candlestick chart to line chart for easy view
3. Look for major reversal areas (areas where price has reversed or supported), mark it up, that might be an area of support and resistance.
4. Look for areas where support turned resistance and resistance turned support, these areas are very important.
5. After drawing your support and resistance, wait for price action, then enter the market if confirmations are met.

I would talk about the confirmation checklist in my other chapter.

NOTE: When drawing your support and resistance always look for higher highs and lower lows.

HOW TO DRAW TREND LINE

1. To draw a trend line, you need a minimum of two points to connect.
2. Draw your line diagonally, this line act as diagonal support and resistance.
3. You can use a rotated rectangle
4. When drawing your trend line, connect the lowest low and the highest high.
5. For an up-trending market, draw your trend line from one low to a higher low or high to higher high.
6. For a down-trending market, draw your trend line from a high to a lower high or low to a lower low.

Fig 14.4

CHAPTER 15
WHAT IS A PULLBACK

OVERVIEW

- What are pullbacks?
- How do you use a pullback to enter the market?

WHAT IS A PULLBACK?

A pullback is a short pause or brief inversion in the value activity of a stock or product. The duration of a pullback is usually only a few consecutive sessions.

Fig 15.1

A longer pause before the uptrend resumes is generally referred to as consolidation.

This is a short term retracement; if you miss an entry, wait for the next pullback and enter.

HOW DO YOU USE PULLBACK TO ENTER THE MARKET

Pullback in terms of technical analysis generates all sorts of trading opportunities after an active trend thrusts higher or lower. Let's outline the most favorable technical conditions for a pullback to turn on a dime as soon as you take a risk in the opposite direction.

- First, you need a strong trend so that other pullback players will be lined up right behind you, ready to jump in and turn your idea into a reliable profit.
- Second, a trending market will always certainly pullback but to what extent would it retraced before the trader enters the market, this is where most traders find it difficult. When a market is trending and you missed entry at the peak of the trend, it's fine because the market will certainly pullback; these pullbacks are where a trader gets a perfect entry, but how do you know the pullback is over.

- Third, am not a fan of indicators and I don't use indicators except for Moving averages, they tell a lot about a trending market. When a trending market starts pulling back they tend to reverse at the moving averages, they act as a guide and help tell when the pullback is over. Most trending market reverses at the 50 EMA, while strong trends with little retracements tend to reverse at the faster moving average such as 21 EMA, 14 EMA, and so on.

  Another tool that's been used and very effective is the FIBONACCI RETRACEMENT TOOL. This is very effective as the price tends to obey it. I would talk more about Fibonacci in my next book. Strong trending market would obey the 38% of the Fibonacci while pulling back, while most times price respect the 61.8% level (this is the golden ratio) when it pulls back. Price also respects support and resistance when trending, during a trending market; if price breaks a support or resistance it always come back to retest that broken support or resistance, this is also a pullback and a trader can find a perfect entry above the support with a stop loss below the support and below the resistance with a stop loss above the resistance. Another tool that can be used to get a perfect entry is a trend line when the market is trending and it pulls back, it pulls back to the trend line giving you a perfect entry and a good risk to reward ratio.

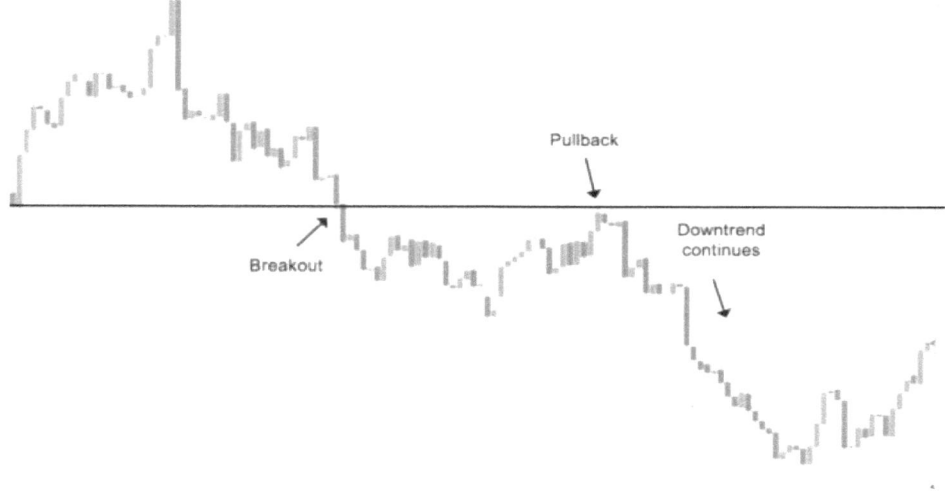

Fig 15.2

CHAPTER 16
CONFIRMATION CHECKLIST

OVERVIEW
- What are 5 confirmations that you use when entering into a market?
- Why do you need confirmation?
- Why do we react to the market and make an effort not to make forecasts?

WHAT ARE WE WATCHING OUT FOR?

There are things you watch out for before entering the market. Traders must lookout for this to get a high probability trade.

- TRENDING
- SUPPORT/RESISTANCE
- CONSOLIDATION
- TRENDLINE
- PRICE MOVING IN THE PROPOSED DIRECTION
- RETEST

- PULLBACKS

Your goal is to take a high probability trade setup; you have to take a good setup to be consistently profitable.

RULES BEFORE ENTERING A TRADE
(1) **Is the market trending?**
- Discover the trend
- Go with the flow
- Look at the higher timeframe

(2) **Support and Resistance[Mandatory]**
- When you note that the market is trending, then you look for support and resistance
- Draw your support and resistance line, areas where support turn resistance and resistance turn support.

(3) **Price Action[Wicks]**
- Wicks tell you a lot about decisions being made in the background.
- Wicks are signs that the market wants to move in the opposite direction.
- When wicks occur in areas of resistance and support or areas of previous resistance and support, this is called a

confluence which is a sign that the market wants to move.
- Look for wicks in major resistance and support areas because this is a sign that the market wants to move the opposite direction.

(4) **Consolidation**
- This is a trader's nightmare.
- This is the market pausing, which is a good indication.
- Consolidation is a good indicator. It indicates that the market either wants to change direction or wants to go up higher.
- Consolidation is good when in conjunction with major support and resistance area. When the market is moving with high momentum and then it pauses, which could be an indication that the market wants to turn around or move higher.

(5) **Trend Lines**
- Did it break or retest the trend line?
- Trend lines are diagonal support and resistance.
- The same way we use support and resistance that is how we use trend lines.

- If price retests the trend line, it means it will continue to go in that direction, but if it breaks the trend line there is a possibility that it is about to change direction.
- We want to see that the market respects the trend line and if at the event of the case is not respecting the trend line that tells us something.

(6) **Price Direction[Mandatory]**
- Look for price to show signs that it wants to go in the direction you think
- If you see that prices at support/resistance have had wicks in the past but currently there is a big fat candle that's currently showing no wicks at all, which means that price was to continue in this direction that it is going which is not the direction I want it to go. Therefore this is not a time to get in.
- But if you see that the prices are going in this direction and it looks like its struggling, the candles are getting smaller, the wicks are getting larger, there is consolidation happening and I see that price is starting to fall just like I want it to. This is the perfect time to enter.

(7) **Retest**
- Look for a retest of support and resistance
- A retest is when price breaks through a support line going down and then comes back to the support line to test that line and act as resistance then continue to fall. This area is a good area to enter for a sell and vice versa for a resistance.
- Do not take a trade unless it retest

(8) **Pullback**
- Whenever you miss a retest, you can enter on pullbacks
- The market must be trending
- Pullback is a good entry and usually occurs during a trending market.

NOTE: *THE TREND IS YOUR FRIEND*

PART 4
RISK AND MONEY MANAGEMENT

CHAPTER 17
TRADING PLAN

OVERVIEW
- Things you should have on your trading plan
- Questions you should be able to answer

The following questions below should be answered by you. As you learn to master the art of trading, these questions will begin to pop out. The answers to these questions are what should make up your trading plan.

(1) WHAT IS YOUR WHY?
- Why do you want to do this?
- Why do you want to win?
- Why do you want this to work?

(2) WHAT TYPE OF TRADER ARE YOU?
- Are you a scalper?
- Are you an intraday trader?
- Are you a swing trader?
- Are you a position trader?

(3) **WHAT TYPE OF STRATEGY DO YOU PREFER?**
- Would give out some strategy that would bring you consistent profit, back-tested and has been proven to be 98% accurate.

(4) **WHAT IS YOUR PRE-TRADING ROUTINE?**
- The things you do before opening your chart to take a trade.
- The things you do before taking any trade matters as they affect your trading results.

(5) **WHAT SESSIONS DO YOU TRADE?**
- The sessions you take your trade matters and should be on your trading plan.
- Is it New York, London, Tokyo session or all of them?

(6) **WHAT SPECIFIC TIME DO YOU TRADE?**
- This should be on your trading plan, you should have a time when you take trades, market moves the most during London/New; you might want to trade during this time.

(7) **BEFORE ENTERING A TRADE, WHAT IS YOUR CRITERIA FOR GETTING IN?**
   - Before entering a trade you should be looking out for confirmations like retest, wicks, pullbacks, trend lines, support, and resistance.

(8) **HOW MANY PIPS DO YOU WANT MINIMUM OUT OF A TRADE?**
   - When in any trade, you should always have a target. This way it won't affect your emotions and you would be able to avoid overtrading.

(9) **HOW MANY PIPS DO YOU WANT TO AVERAGE A WEEK....EVENTUALLY?**
   - This is your pip target for the week; you would be able to know your consistency in a profitable trade.

(10) **WHAT PERCENT OF YOUR ACCOUNT ARE YOU WILLING TO RISK?**
   - This question should be answered by you and should be in your trading plan. This would go a long way in managing your risk. Most newbie traders have blown account justs because they were not able

to manage their risk properly. You can't have a $100 account and use a lot size of 0.05 and expect not to blow this account, you would blow this account as a newbie. You ought not to risk over 3% of your account.

(11) WHAT PERCENT OF YOUR ACCOUNT ARE YOU WILLING TO RISK IN A DAY/WEEK?

- The amount of your money you want to risk in a week, this should be in your trading plan.

(12) HOW WILL YOU MANAGE THE TRADE ONCE YOU GET IN IT?

- What decision would you take when in a trade?
- How many times would you check your trade, every one hour, every four hours, every 15 minutes?
- What would you do if you are in a drawdown, how do you react?
- Do you break even once in profit and by how many pips?

(13) WHAT IS YOUR EXIT STRATEGY?

- Do you trail your stop loss?

- Do you wait for the price to hit your take profit target?
- Do you take partials before the price hits your take profit target?

(14) HOW MUCH TRADING WILL YOU DO A DAY/WEEK/MONTH

- Do not overtrade to avoid too much loss
- Always set a stop loss, let it hit your stop loss.

(15) DESCRIBE YOUR IDEAL TRADE SETUP?

- A giant red cow standing amid other white cows.

(16) WHAT CURRENCY PAIRS WILL YOU TRADE?

- Do you have pairs you won't trade?
- If a pair constitutes most of your losses, either you stop trading that pair or you learn how it moves.
- If you love a pair, then trade it and master it.

(17) WHAT DAYS/WEEKS/SEASONS WILL YOU NOT TRADE?
- Example: Holidays, sessions, downtimes
- Would you take trades on Mondays and Fridays?
- Would you take trades when it's NFP Friday? All this should be in your trading plan.

(18) HOW MANY POSITIONS WILL YOU HAVE OPEN UP AT ANY GIVEN TIME?
- How many pairs will you open at a given time?
- How many positions of the same pair will you open at the same time

(19) WHAT WILL YOU DO FOR PERSONAL DEVELOPMENT?
- What books will you read?
- Would you go to the Gym?
- What would you do when you have consecutive losses?
- What actions would you take when you have a bad trading week?

(20) WHAT WILL YOU DO WITH THE MONEY YOU MAKE FROM TRADING?

- Would you save part of the money?
- Would you invest part of the money?
- Would you give tithes in the church?
- Would you pay tax?
- How much are you willing to use for your expenses?

(21) HOW WILL YOU KEEP RECORDS OF YOUR TRADE?

- As a trader, you should have a trading journal
- When using a trading journal, it helps you make decisions and helps you figure out what you have been doing wrong.

(22) HOW OFTEN WILL YOU MONITOR YOUR TRADE?

- Don't babysit your trade
- Set alerts when you want to check your trade
- Am not going to check it every 2 hours
- Am not going to check it every 5 hours
- Am only going to check it once a day

CHAPTER 18
RISK MANAGEMENT PART 1

OVERVIEW
- What is meant by proper risk management?
- How do I use the position size calculator

In the monetary world, risk management is the process of identification, investigation, and acceptance or acknowledgment of uncertainty in investment decisions. Inadequate risk management can result to severe cases like blowing of account, accruing big losses, etc. Most newbie traders don't last in this industry due to improper risk management and they end up blowing their account several times thinking it's the strategy.

I will tell you today that no strategy is Holy Grail; there isn't any holy grail in forex. As long as you are a trade, be ready to welcome losses. Proper risk management is what will keep you in the industry for a long time.

Risk only 1-3% of the total account on one currency pair. You are only in control of how much you can lose.

CORRECT STOPS FOR THE TYPE OF TRADE TAKEN

S/N	TYPE	PERIOD	PIPS
1	SCALP	FEW MINUTES	1-10 PIPS
2	INTRADAY	FEW HOURS	10-40 PIPS
3	DAY	1-2 DAYS	20-40 PIPS
4	SWING	1+ WEEKS	80-250 PIPS
5	POSITION	1+ MONTHS	200-600+ PIPS

HOW TO USE POSITION SIZE CALCULATOR

- Type "position size calculator" on google
- Click on "myfxbook.com"
- Use the above site to calculate your position size

NOTE: Not every trade is for everyone! It depends on your account size, which is why I don't advise Beginners to engage in signals, it's the fastest way to blow your account. I am talking from experience.

WHAT IT TAKES TO USE 0.05 LOT WITH 3% RISK

S/N	TYPE	DEPOSIT	STOP
1	SCALPER	$100	6
2	INTRADAY	$500	30
3	DAY	$1000	60
4	SWING	$2000	120
5	POSITION	$5000	300

CHAPTER 19
RISK MANAGEMENT PART 2

OVERVIEW

- How do I open up positions and how many should I open to reflect good risk management.
- How to break one trade position into multiple trade positions
- What is meant by risk to reward ratio
- What is meant by not every trade is for everybody
- What are correlated pairs?

TWIN TRADING AND TRIPLET TRADING

This is the act of breaking your trades into multiple positions and still keep good risk management.

When you want to open more positions on a particular pair and still maintain good risk management, divide the total lot size by the number of trade you want to open. E.g. If you decide to use 0.5 lot size and open two positions, then you would use 0.25 lot size respectively for the two positions.

GOOD RISK MANAGEMENT

If you want to trade GBPJPY, let's assume risking 3% of your account is 0.066 lot size.

PAIR	LOT SIZE	%RISK
GBPJPY	0.033	1.5%
GBPJPY	0.033	1.5%
TOTAL	0.066	3%

BAD RISK MANAGEMENT

Lets still use the above example;

PAIR	LOT SIZE	%RISK
GBPJPY	0.066	3%
GBPJPY	0.066	3%
TOTAL	0.132	6%

So instead of risking 3%, you risk 6% which is bad risk management.

- Always diversify your trades
- Get a journal and keep track of all your Buy/Sell and Win/Losses
- There should be no more than 4 open positions of the same pair at the same time
- Do not trade too many pairs with the same currency at the same time, they can all be affected. Example: NZDCHF, NZDJPY, EURNZD, GBPNZD……. If NZD is affected, it will affect all of them. When NZDCHF is in loss, all your trade will go into loss because they all have NZD.
- Do not take trades that are positively correlated at the same time. For example; AUDUSD, EURUSD, NZDUSD, GBPUSD, these pairs are positively correlated and will move in the same direction, it is not safe to take these trades all at once.

- Correlated pairs are pairs that have similar movements in the same direction.
- Let your risk to reward ratio be greater or equal to 1:1

RISK	REWARD	RATIO	RATE
35pips	15pips	0.42:1	Bad
35pips	35pips	1:1	Good
35pips	70pips	1:2	Better

CONCLUSION

I have been educating and trading the financial market for over six years. The one thing I always like to point out when I am talking to my many students is that there is no "Holy Grail" of trading. I often run into traders who think that they can buy FOREX trading software and use it like an ATM just put in a pin, and pops out the cash. It just doesn't work that way.

This is a real market. It is the largest financial market in the world, and you have to treat it as such. You can trade this market part-time, or you can do it every day.

The real "Holy Grail," if any, is inside your brain, in conjunction with your psychological awareness and control and the cumulative experience and knowledge you have acquired and the alignment of your goals and your actions in harmony and perfection through a good amount of practice, then again practice, and then again more practice until knowledge transforms into intuitive wisdom.

Trading can be learned, of course, but the experience can't be transmitted.

It has to be constructed by every individual through a personal effort of understanding and hard work. It will not happen overnight. Trading needs a similar dedication as any precision-driven career. The theory is good, but practice makes perfect and integrates all the knowledge you have acquired.

Another thing that is important to understand is that you will never stop learning. Markets are changing every day, and the FOREX is a living organism that evolves in the same way as all its traders. Always remember that although it seems to be an anonymous entity, at the end of the day, the market is merely made up of investors, large and small, from all corners of the world, each with his or her own emotions, psychology, and predictable behaviors and reactions.

As I asked earlier, how long does a doctor, lawyer, engineer, or any other regulated professional have to go to school to learn his or her trade?

Some of these individuals literally could be in school for 10 years just learning to be good at what they do, and that doesn't include any practical experience. Wow! That's a long time; to be a FOREX trader is no different.

Okay, you don't have to go to school for 10 years, but you do have to put in your "seat time" on the computer.

You will have to invest in your education; you will have to seek out knowledge and someone who can help you learn to trade this market. I hope that after reading this book, you will easily decide that I am the person from whom you want to learn more.

In the FOREX and life as well, this will be very useful to you. Keep it simple and straight (KISS)!

Learn to move on after losses. Don't dwell on missed trades or missed pips after you decide to close. There will be hundreds of opportunities in the future. Follow your plan, and follow your system. Practice every day, and experience will come with time, patience, and discipline. Don't look outside for what's already inside. Leave your ego behind; be humble and smart. You can't decide where the market will go, so learn to see where it wants to lead you, not the other way around. Exit bad trades, and hold onto good trades. Set yourself a goal, and stop trading when you have reached it.

STRATEGIES THAT WORK 80% OF THE TIME

- **THE ULTIMATE KILL**

This strategy is indicator based and works 80% of the time.

WHAT IS NEEDED
- Bollinger bands(default setting)
- RSI(default setting)

We use the 15m, 30m, H1, and H4 timeframe

STEP 1
Check if the price is touching the Bollinger bands (upper or lower) for all timeframe mentioned above; if all the timeframes align then you are good to go, if no don't bother entering the market.

STEP 2
Check if RSI is above 70 or below 30 for 15m, 30m, H1, and H4; remember they must all align, if you see this then it is a good setup, if not don't bother trading.

STEP 3
Check FOREXFACTORY.COM for red folder;
Go to forexfactory.com, Check under calendar and you would see currencies that have major news for that day. If a currency has a red folder, then don't trade any pair that has that currency, if there is no red folder for either of the currencies in the pair you want to trade then you are good to go.

NOTE: If all conditions are met, then trade with your stop-loss above the Bollinger band for a sell and below the Bollinger bands for a buy.

STEP 4
Break even when in profit and have a take profit of 30 pips.

NOTE: These conditions must meet for all the timeframe I mentioned.

NOTE: When the price is touching the upper Bollinger band and RSI is above 70, we are going to sell; when the price is touching the lower Bollinger band and RSI is below 30, we are going to buy.

- ***BREAK AND RETEST***

This strategy is purely naked trading and will give a return of 90% accuracy.

STEP 1
Change your candlestick chart to a line chart

STEP 2
Observe where the price is and where it might be heading to.

STEP 3
Look to your left and check for where price reversed (that is where price reversed and changed direction)

STEP 4
Draw your support line and resistance line putting in mind where the price is.

NOTE: Support and resistance can be a zone

STEP 5
Observe what the current price is doing and wait for a breakout.

STEP 6
After breakout don't enter the market, this is where the market makers do some fake-out to the retail traders, instead wait for a retest of that breakout.

STEP 7
When the retest occurs, enter the market with your stop-loss below the resistance area for a buy and above the support for a sell.

STEP 8
Have a profit target of 30 pips and once in profit break even.

THANK YOU

www.ingramcontent.com/pod-product-compliance
Lightning Source LLC
Chambersburg PA
CBHW021417210526
45463CB00001B/413